The Joy of Motherhood

Karen Lancaster Brown

Meadowbrook Press

Distributed by Simon & Schuster
New York

Library of Congress Cataloging-in-Publication Data

Brown, Karen (Lancaster)
  The joy of motherhood / by Karen Lancaster Brown.
      p. cm.
  ISBN 0-88166-467-7 (Meadowbrook), ISBN 0-684-02144-7 (Simon & Schuster)
  1. Mothers—Quotations, maxims, etc. 2. Motherhood—Quotations,
maxims, etc. I. Title.

  PN6084.M6B76 2004
  306.874'3—dc22

                          2003018729

Editor: Bruce Lansky
Editorial Director: Christine Zuchora-Walske
Coordinating Editors: Kelsey Anderson and Megan McGinnis
Editorial Assistant: Signe Peterson
Production Manager: Paul Woods
Graphic Design Manager: Tamara Peterson
Cover Photography: © Francisco Cruz/SuperStock
Interior Photography: © Brand X Pictures

Published by Meadowbrook Press, 5451 Smetana Drive, Minnetonka, Minnesota 55343
www.meadowbrookpress.com

BOOK TRADE DISTRIBUTION by Simon and Schuster, a division of Simon and Schuster, Inc.,
1230 Avenue of the Americas, New York, NY 10020

09 08 07 06 05 04   10 9 8 7 6 5 4 3 2 1

Printed in the United States of America

Dedication

To my mother, Betty Lancaster,
and my son, Barrett Brown,
with love.

Acknowledgments

We'd like to thank the people who served on a reading panel for this project: Becky Bowman, Tasha Brewer, Carolyne Cooper, Sandra de los Rios, Susan Erne, Amy Gaillard, Sharon Hamilton, Kathleen Josephson, Amy Maikkula, Cindy Roers, Pearl Saban, Naomi Saccavino, Kathryn White, Kimberly Wouters, Brenda Yeand, and especially Christy Karmanos.

Introduction

In French, the word is *mère*. In Russian, *mat*, and
in Spanish, *madre*. But whatever language you're speaking,
the universal definition for *mother* would always include
love—the truest love there is, a love that crosses
boundaries and lasts a lifetime.

The old saying goes, "God could not be everywhere.
That's why he created mothers." And for those of us lucky
enough to have had that relationship, we know it's true.

If you are a mother, have a mother,
or hope to be one someday, I hope you'll find
something here to serve as your own personal
tribute to mothers everywhere.

Karen Brown

Karen Lancaster Brown

When you hold your newborn,
you've got the whole world in your hands.

∞

A mom gives birth not only to a child,
but also to a future.

At her child's birth,
a woman is reborn into her
new life as a mother.

ᐸᐳ

New mothers hope to go gently
into that good night—and get a few
hours of uninterrupted sleep.

ᐸᐳ

A mother and her child
mirror each other's souls.

Motherhood is a gift that keeps on giving.

⚮

Your newborn?
Heaven has sent you one of its angels.

⚮

New mothers remember to count
their blessings—right after they've counted
their newborns' fingers and toes.

You've come a long way, baby,
when your newborn starts sleeping
through the night.

⟨⟩

Nothing's free—except a mother's love.

Motherhood is a lifelong
promise—a promise of encouragement,
support, and most of all, love.

❧

A fool for love:
a mom with her newborn.

❧

Your heart stops
as you gaze upon the face
of your newborn child.

To a baby, Mother's face
is the best entertainment.

e×ɔ

A mother can see the future
in her child's eyes.

e×ɔ

It's easy to know what
mothers should do—until
you become one.

To sleep, perchance to dream?
Moms of newborns can only fantasize.

Moms of newborns often find
the best diet by default—they just don't
have the time or energy to eat.

A baby's needs are simple:
milk, warmth, love—and all can
be found in Mother's arms.

❧

The heart of the matter:
a mother's love.

❧

Moms give with no strings
attached—except heartstrings.

A child's first love is always Mother.

c✕ɔ

The well of mother-love never runs dry.

c✕ɔ

Sleep like a baby:
Once you become a mother,
you never misuse that phrase again!

Mothers understand the silent
language of a warm embrace.

૯✕૭

Moms of fussy babies quickly learn
how to do everything with one hand.

૯✕૭

Motherhood is an opportunity to both
raise a child and grow up yourself.

A mom knows *everyone's* gonna
get wet when it's baby's bath time.

⌒

A new mom's favorite lullaby?
"Rock-a-Dry Baby."

With each new baby,
a mother writes a new chapter
in her book of love.

cxɔ

Dream a little dream:
Envision life's opportunities
with your child.

First-time moms of newborns
often find themselves waiting for
the "real" mom to step in.

⚬

Becoming a mother helps you
put things in perspective.

New moms appreciate
the support of other moms.
After all, maternity is a sorority.

∝

Motherhood is a celebration
of life and love.

Rock around the clock?
It takes on a whole new meaning
for moms of fussy babies.

⌒✕⌒

New moms quickly learn
not to cry over spilled milk—or
apple juice, for that matter.

⌒✕⌒

What's a new mom's favorite scent?
Eau de baby lotion.

It's a beautiful moment
when your infant first smiles at you.

☙

For mothers of babies,
playing peekaboo never gets old.

A mother needs her own
time-out chair—or at least
a bed and a good book.

☙

A simple "I love you, Mommy"
is the key to unlock a mother's heart.

☙

Mothers give from the heart
and expect nothing in return.

Motherhood is a net of love
that grows stronger as it stretches.

c×ɔ

A child will do what Mother does,
not what she says.

Managing a stressful career
is nothing compared to handling a child's
tantrum in a crowded grocery store.

⤫

Who are we kidding?
All mothers are working mothers!

⤫

Don't worry about potty training.
It all comes out in the end.

Moms know how the
cookie crumbles—that's why
they have DustBusters.

∞

Mom's bag of tricks in a house of worship:
1. Roll of Life Savers
2. Pencil and paper
3. *Sh!*
4. "Just wait till we get home!"

Essential job skill for motherhood:
the ability to read bedtime stories with a
different voice for each character.

☙

Children should be seen and not heard?
Whoever thought that one up
obviously didn't love children.

A child's hug can warm
your heart and feed your soul.

໐✕໐

When the writing's on the wall,
it's usually all over the carpet, too.

Motherhood is made up of small
sacrifices—and big rewards.

ℰↃ

To a child, nothing is worse than
a disappointed look from Mother.

ℰↃ

When your toddler asks you, "Why?"
for the tenth time, remember that in ten years,
he may stop speaking to you altogether.

Moms of toddlers know all the
best public restrooms in town.

cx

Moms of two-year-olds must remember:
Growing up is hard to do.

A good mom shares her umbrella
during a storm and helps her child
see the rainbow afterward.

⁓

A mother's love may
not prevent injury—but it can
certainly ease the pain.

Mothers' words of encouragement
are often the boost children need
to reach their goals.

c×ɔ

Smart moms remember
that their kids are only young once.

c×ɔ

Wise moms encourage
kids to color outside the lines.

Your mom always said
you'd appreciate her someday.
And now that you're a mom
yourself, you really do.

∞

A mother's love doesn't
have to be earned.

Building strong children is much
easier than fixing weak ones.

∽

When your child hurts, *you* hurt.

A toddler's awe reminds
us to stop and notice life's
everyday miracles.

⟡

It's not until we have
our own children that we fully
appreciate our mothers.

Wise mothers often thumb
their noses at convention.

c×𝜕

When does your little one
need a bedtime drink of water?
The moment you've gotten
comfortable on the sofa.

A mother knows when
her child needs to laugh
to keep from crying.

❧

For moms, little things—like
peanut-butter-scented kisses and
sleepy hugs—mean a lot.

Grateful moms see the small blessings
in days full of wiping runny noses,
fixing peanut butter sandwiches,
and kissing scraped knees.

c×ɔ

A mother's hug can
heal almost any wound.

From the mouths of babes
will come some of your most
embarrassing moments.

∞

Smart moms know it's better to
hold one's temper than to lose it.

A mother is there when
you need someone to lean on.

☙☘☙

Clever moms figure out ways
to convince their children to try vegetables
without power struggles.

When a child's ready to boil over,
a mom knows how to turn down the heat.

$c \times 0$

Mothers love their children *for*
themselves—not *in spite of* themselves.

Oh, the places you'll
go—like behind the bush at the side
of the road—with a toddler.

⌒×⌒

A mother's most priceless
gift is forgiveness.

A mother's three steps to compromise:
1. Not now.
2. I mean it.
3. Oh, okay.

❧

Moms know that even
the most rambunctious children
look like angels when asleep.

Wise moms remember
that the years for sweet bedtime
stories are numbered.

◦✕◦

You're not getting out enough
when playing the "quiet game" becomes
your favorite activity.

◦✕◦

One of the saddest times for a mom?
When her child wants to read
a bedtime story alone.

Creative moms do their best work
in the kitchen, disguising all kinds of
vegetables with cheese sauce.

∞

Left holding the bag?
Run after the school bus
with your kid's lunch.

A mother does whatever it takes
to bring out the best in her children.

❧

Blessed is the mother who knows when
to speak—and when to remain silent.

Sometimes a mother's
job is just to be there, listen,
and offer a hug.

⌒

Wise moms know that yesterday's
mistakes are today's lessons.

Helpful moms remind their kids
that after a big disappointment,
tomorrow's a new day.

A mother can make
her home a fortress of love in
a sometimes-scary world.

∞

Mothers are the glue that
holds families together.

Many things are better left unsaid,
but wise moms know words of praise,
encouragement, and love are
not among them.

_c✗ɔ_

Busy mothers know
you really can't *find* time.
You have to *make* it.

When the kitchen is a mess, remember that you're not just making cookies with your child—you're making memories.

cↄ

A mother is stingy with criticism and generous with praise.

cↄ

Home is where the mom is—and thus where the heart is.

Smart moms tell their kids
that it's better to lose a race with dignity
than to win with dishonesty.

❧

Busy moms call a bucket-of-chicken dinner
"cuisine à la drive-through."

❧

Moms spin the threads of love
that bind a family's hearts together.

Mothers know everything about
their kids—and love them anyway.

☙

Smart moms make sure
their kids get the recommended daily
allowance of hugs, kisses, and TLC.

A mother's love can lighten the load.

A good mother doesn't serve
as a crutch. She teaches her child
how to walk through life.

Wise moms stop and think
before giving their children the go-ahead.

⁕

A smart mom reminds her child
that mistakes are just proof of trying.

A wise mom honors her child's opinion,
even if she doesn't share it.

cxɔ

Mothers know that there's never
a wrong time to do the right thing.

cxɔ

A mother will go the extra mile
with her child—even on an unpaved road.

A mom will stop at nothing
when it comes to doing the right thing
for her child.

෧

A mother knows her child's faults
are nobody else's business.

Mother of invention?
She's the one who can create a superhero
costume out of old scarves.

⚬✕⚬

Proud moms will show you
that the past is full of Kodak moments.

Is watching *Harry Potter
and the Chamber of Secrets* for the
fourteenth time with your kid "quality time"?
Yes, if you both enjoy it.

✎

Cook, teacher, nurse,
and friend—a mom does it all.

When kids feel like marching
to a different drummer, smart
moms join the parade.

❧

Behind every blue-ribbon winner
is a cheering mother.

Though a mother wants
to say yes always, she loves her
child enough to say no often.

C⤬Ɔ

A good mother gives her child
a map to the roads of life.

The more the merrier?
Not when it comes to six-year-olds
drinking red Kool-Aid in your den.

∞

The best thing about a
conversation with a wise mother
is that she really listens.

A wise mom teaches her child to
cross only the bridge directly ahead—and
to not burn any bridge left behind.

☙❧

So what if it's carpool time
and you're still in your robe and slippers?
Ready or not, here you come.

When children have cold feet,
a mother's encouragement feels
like warm slippers.

❧

A mother's sweet words can chase
away the bitter taste of disappointment.

Got milk? Add a few cookies.

⤫

Smart moms know
that fun with the kids is always more
important than a clean house.

⤫

When all else fails,
an ice-cream sundae can
stop the bickering.

A mother is there when you
need someone to lean on.

લ✕૭

Wise moms know
that trips with the kids can't
really be called vacations.

A mother's love is a candle
that lights up the dark places
in her child's life.

cxɔ

Good mothers know the difference
between hearing and listening.

cxɔ

Love begins at home—and
it usually returns there.

Many a mom wears the pants
in the family—and pays for them, too.

∽

Supportive moms cheer their kids,
whether leading the pack or bringing
up the rear, across the finish line.

A wise mom urges her child
to keep trying in trying times.

⌀

A child has the right to remain silent,
except when Mom is standing there
waiting for an answer.

Smart moms know that it's
work—and not just words—that
helps kids reach their goals.

❧

Behind every successful person
is a mother who wouldn't listen
to the words *I give up*.

A mother is a sounding board
for her child's hopes and fears.

ⅇ✕⅁

Smart moms teach their children
that the best thing about always telling
the truth is that you never have
to remember what you said.

Moms teach their kids
that when push comes to shove,
words are the best weapons.

☙❧

Tough love—it's not for softies.

☙❧

A wise mom always tries to see
things from her child's point of view.

Childhood stories get better
each time a mother retells them.

c⨯ɔ

When a kid's stuck
between a rock and a hard place,
Mom's the perfect crowbar.

c⨯ɔ

Kids cherish their moms'
ability to remember—and to forget.

Mothers know that the
seeds of discipline can be bitter,
but the harvest is sweet.

⌒⌒

Smart mothers don't smother.

⌒⌒

When a child's fishing for compliments,
Mom will always bite.

When the bread falls
on the floor butter side down,
guess who usually cleans up?

cᐁ

A child with his mom behind him?
Now, that's a winning team.

A mother can't prevent her
child from doing wrong, but she can
keep her kid from enjoying it.

❧

A smart mom hitches
her wagon to a carpool.

A mother provides roots
for the most important seedling
she'll ever nurture.

cx

Smart moms make the most
of their time with their kids before
most of the time is gone.

Eat, drink, and be merry—when
the kids are away at a sleepover.

∞

The things we do for love
(like staying up all night to finish
that fabulous costume for your
child's school play)!

When a preteen daughter
first applies makeup, it's a face
only a mother could love.

ᐸ✕ᐳ

Kids can count on their
mothers to walk in when everyone
else has walked out.

Children know they're in
trouble when their mothers call
them by their full names.

∞

Smart moms are thrifty with
money spent on their kids—and
lavish with attention.

There's no place
like home—especially
when mom's there, waiting
with open arms.

Mothers who seek happiness
for their children often find
it for themselves.

⌒⌒

Mothers know that love
is the most important building
material for a strong
and solid home.

A smart mom doesn't insist
on seeing everything her way.
She lets her kids use their own eyes.

∽

Between mothers and
their children, love *does* mean
having to say you're sorry.

Smart moms keep the pizza delivery
phone number on speed dial.

⌒×⌒

As a mom, you quickly learn
that it's no fun when your child is
grounded—because you're
grounded, too!

Realistic moms know that
if they tell their kids something once,
they may have to tell them
a thousand times.

c×ɔ

Aging moms know that
wrinkles are just evidence of years of
laughter—and moments of tears.

Wise moms don't mind
dropping off their teens a block
away from school.

ℯ⤬ꝺ

Mothers of teens learn to judge
the deed—not the doer.

ℯ⤬ꝺ

It's not the destination that matters;
it's the journey—especially when your
teen gets his driver's license.

No news is good news?
Not when your teen's out past curfew.

c⌀⌁

Wise moms fasten their seatbelts
when their children hit puberty.
It's going to be a bumpy ride.

c⌀⌁

Mothers help their children celebrate
successes—and learn from failures.

When a child loses the way in life,
a mother can serve as a compass.

C✕ↄ

A smart mom tells you
what you *need* to hear, not
what you *want* to hear.

Remember how much your mom
hated *your* hair, clothes, and music
when you were a teenager?

☙

Seeing is believing:
when that rebellious teen returns
from college for the first time and
is so happy to be with you.

Fools and their money are
soon parted—especially when your
teen gets that first paycheck.

※

It's shocking when you hear
your mother's words coming from your
mouth—and they sound so right!

※

The best mothers lead by example.

Adolescents look to mom
for a tie that binds, but not too tightly.

❧

Mothers help their children reach
for the stars—and make sure their feet
are planted firmly on the ground.

❧

Boldly go where no one has gone before.
Clean under your teen's bed.

You don't want to stifle your kid's creativity—except when you spot a bottle of purple hair dye in the bathroom right before college interviews.

c⤬⤮

The son also rises—but on Saturdays, not until noon.

Whatever mothers do
or say embarrasses teens.
Don't take it personally.

౭✕౨

A mother is in the
driver's seat only until her oldest
gets his learner's permit.

Moms often cry when their kids
go off to college—and when their
kids move back home again.

❧

The same children who often
give you gray hairs will be a comfort
when you're completely gray.

Smart moms tell their kids
that loose behavior can put
them in a tight situation.

cx⌀

From diapers to driver's
licenses, moms know it's better
to be safe than sorry.

Wearing clean underwear in case
of an accident? Heck, you just hope
your teen is wearing *any*.

☙

All good things must come to an end:
Every well-behaved child will
eventually hit puberty.

Also from Meadowbrook Press

The Joy of…Series

Six treasuries of wise and warm advice for that special parent, grandparent, spouse, sister, or friend in your life. These collections reflect the wittiest and wisest (and sometimes most amusing) sentiments ever written about those whom we hold most dear. These books are the perfect gift to show a loved one how much you care. *The Joy of Cats*, *The Joy of Friendship*, *The Joy of Grandparenting*, *The Joy of Marriage*, *The Joy of Parenthood*, and *The Joy of Sisters*.

Getting Your Child from No to Yes

By understanding why children say no, and by using the encouraging strategies from *Getting Your Child from No to Yes*, parents can build positive relationships with their children based on trust and unconditional love. Each chapter includes helpful hints and scripts to help parents learn what to say to their children when conflicts arise.

Look Who's Talking!

Using the latest academic research, Laura Dyer, MCD, has written the most comprehensive book available that shows parents how to enhance their children's language development, starting at birth.

**We offer many more titles written to delight, inform, and entertain.
To order books with a credit card or browse our full
selection of titles, visit our website at:**

www.meadowbrookpress.com

or call toll-free to place an order, request a free catalog, or ask a question:

1-800-338-2232

Meadowbrook Press • 5451 Smetana Drive • Minnetonka, MN • 55343